Inside and Underground

CONTENTS

NATIONAL GEOGRAPHIC   Hampton-Brown

School Publishing

Words with Long o

o_e

Look at each picture. Read the words.

Example:

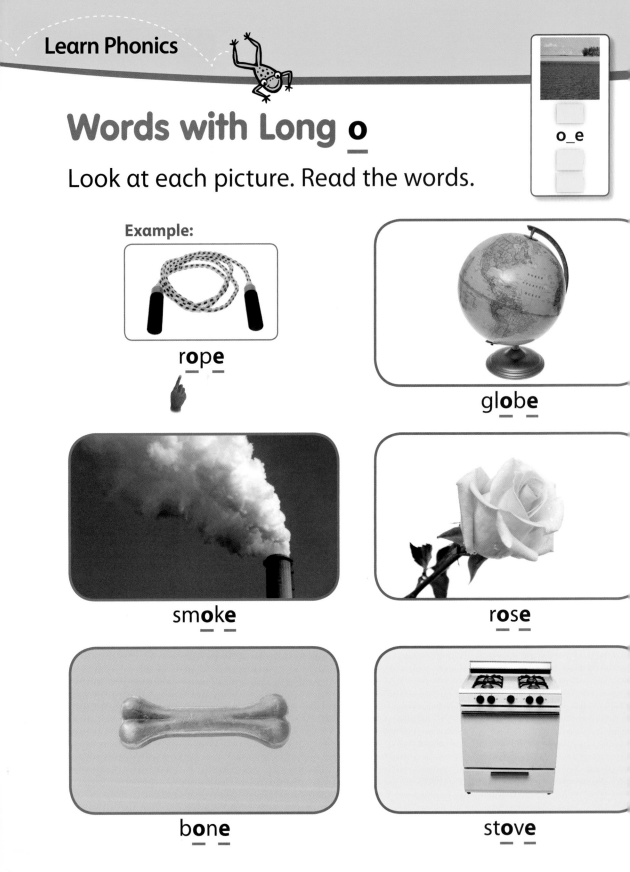

rope

globe

smoke

rose

bone

stove

High Frequency
Words
| always |
| any |
| each |
| every |
| many |
| never |

Key Words

Look at the picture. Read the sentences.

The Mole and the Cat

1. Moles can dig **many** holes.
2. This cat **always** wants to catch a mole.
3. But she **never** catches **any** .
4. **Each** and **every** time a mole smells a cat, it hides.

Where do moles always live?

The Mole

by Carlos Santo

illustrated by Susan Reaga

pink nose

soft, black fuzz

pink toes

This is a mole. It has soft,
black fuzz. It has a pink nose
and pink toes.

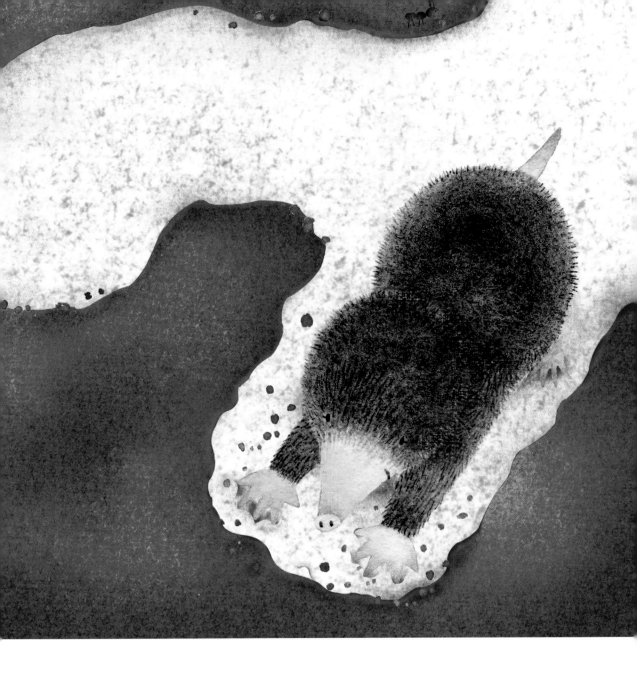

Those toes can dig. Those little
toes dig many big holes.

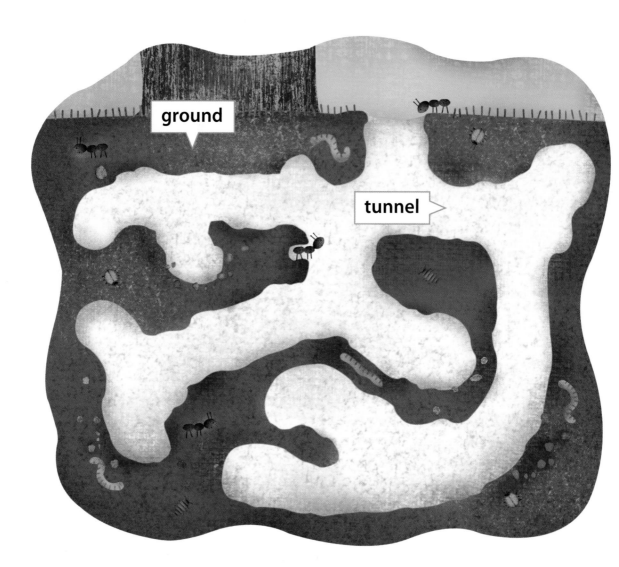

This is a mole's home. It's a
tunnel. Each tunnel is a long hole
in the ground.

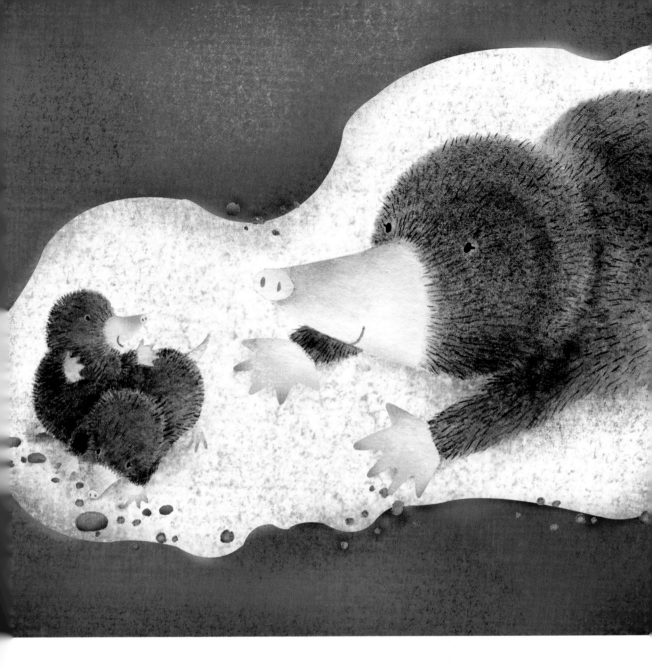

Every little mole lives in a tunnel
with its mother. When a mole grows
up, it makes a home.

A mole's nose helps it catch
slugs. Sniff, sniff! The mole smells
a slug for lunch.

Moles never like to see you.
A mole can poke its nose up at
any time.

But if it sees you, ZIP!

It always runs home. ❖

Words with Long o

Read these words.

rope	nose	bone	like
stone	bite	hose	not

Find the words with long **o**.
Use letters to build them.

r o p e

Talk Together

Choose words from the box
above to talk to a partner about moles.

There's a rope in Mole's hole.

More Words with Long o

Look at each picture. Read the words.

Example:

s**o** little

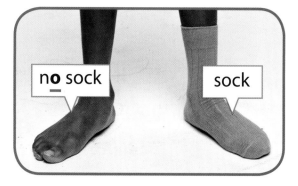

n**o** sock   sock

s**o** big

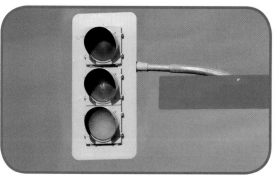

g**o**

Do not g**o**.

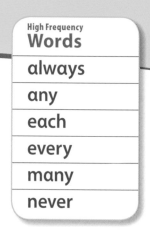

High Frequency Words

always
any
each
every
many
never

Key Words

Read the sentences. Match each sentence to one of the pictures.

Kangaroos

1. **Many** kangaroos come here **every** day.
2. **Each** mother kangaroo **always** has her little one with her.
3. **Every** kangaroo has two strong back legs.
4. **Never** stand too close to **any** kangaroo!

How does a mother kangaroo carry her little one?

Phonics Games

NGReach.com

13

Kangaroos

by Kate Pershing

pouch

A mother kangaroo always has a pouch. She takes her baby with her in the pouch.

A pouch is like a pocket. The
mother never lets the baby run off.
The baby is always safe.

back legs

Every kangaroo has two big back
legs. The legs can jump and kick.
Each time the kangaroo jumps, the
baby will go bump, bump!

little legs

Every kangaroo has two little legs.

Kangaroos eat many kinds of plants.

The little legs grab the plants to eat.

Kangaroos rest in the shade. They play and they eat in the shade, too.

This little kangaroo left its
mother's pouch. It is so big, it can't
fit. It can't go in the pouch any more.

This kangaroo has no baby in its pouch. But some day it will. Now it can still go bump, bump! ❖

More Words with Long o

Read these words.

so	no	got	fast
go	on	big	little

Find the words with long **o**. Use letters to build words.

s　o

Talk Together

Choose words from the box above to tell your partners about kangaroos.

The kangaroo is _so_ _big_.

Kangaroo Is Lost

Play with a partner. Help a kangaroo find its mother. Take turns reading the clues. Trace the path with your finger.

1. Go where there are many stones.
2. Hop over each big hole.
3. Jump over every rope. Don't miss any.
4. Never stop. Go home to Mother.

Acknowledgments

Grateful acknowledgment is given to the authors, artists, photographers, museums, publishers, and agents for permission to reprint copyrighted material. Every effort has been made to secure the appropriate permission. If any omissions have been made or if corrections are required, please contact the Publisher.

Photographic Credits

CVR (Cover) Tony Evans/Timelaps/Taxi/Getty Images. **2** (bl) PhotoDisc/Getty Images. (br) PhotoDisc/Getty Images. (cl) Carole Castelli/Shutterstock. (cr) Lijuan Guo/Shutterstock. (tl) WestLight/iStockphoto. (tr) morganl/iStockphoto. **3** (b) Liz Garza Williams/Hampton-Brown/ National Geographic School Publishing. **11** (t) Liz Garza Williams/Hampton-Brown/National Geographic School Publishing. **12** (bl) Andrew Park/Shutterstock. (br) Sue Smith/iStockphoto. (tl) Sphotos/iStockphoto. (tr) urosr/Shutterstock. **13** (b) Liz Garza Williams/Hampton-Brown/ National Geographic School Publishing. (tc) Rusty Dodson/iStockphoto. (tl) Dave Watts/NHPA/ Photoshot. (tr) blickwinkel/Alamy Images. **14** Martin Rugner/age fotostock/Photolibrary. **15** Sarah Salmela/Shutterstock. **16** Mitsuaki Iwago/Minden Pictures/National Geographic Image Collection. **17** Frans Lanting/Encyclopedia/Corbis. **18** Bob Stefko /The Image Bank/Getty Images. **19** Martin Rugner/age fotostock. **20** Christopher Meder/iStockphoto. **21** (t) Liz Garza Williams/Hampton-Brown/National Geographic School Publishing.

Illustrator Credits

3, 11, 21, 22-23 Jim Paillot; **4-10** Susan Reagan

The National Geographic Society

John M. Fahey, Jr., President & Chief Executive Officer
Gilbert M. Grosvenor, Chairman of the Board

National Geographic School Publishing
Hampton-Brown
www.NGSP.com

Printed in the USA.
RR Donnelley, Jefferson City, MO

ISBN:978-0-7362-8036-5

13 14 15 16 17 18 19
10 9 8 7 6